Kids Make
Christmas

Over 40 kids' craft projects for Christmas

Pia Deges

David and Charles

www.stitchcraftcreate.co.uk

Contents

Tips & tricks on pages 4 and 5

Templates start on page 100

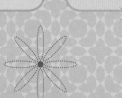

Tips & tricks

Remember!

- Whether you are working on the floor or at the table, always make sure that everything is well covered. Old newspapers, cardboard boxes, waterproof tablecloths and even cut-open bin liners are ideal.

- Place a few cloths out ready, in case something goes wrong or your fingers get sticky.

- Paper plates are perfect for mixing acrylic paints. Wear disposable gloves to make sure that it is only your models and not your fingers that are colourful!

- Kebab sticks and toothpicks are ideal for sticking things down so that they are easier to paint. They are also great for applying small amounts of glue or paint or for sticking fiddly small parts (like sequins and googly eyes) in place.

- Hot-melt glue guns and knives must always be used by adults!

- Left-over Christmas wrapping paper and fabric scraps can be used for all sorts of projects.

Making templates

You can find templates for many of the projects at the back of the book. You will need to copy them to the desired size where marked up. Once you have done this, you can get started with your templates. Place a sheet of tracing paper over your chosen pattern and trace over all the parts you need using a pencil.

You can now stick the tracing paper onto light photo paper and neatly cut out your parts. It is best to use scissors or a craft knife.

Next, place your template the wrong way around onto the photo paper and draw around the outline again with a pencil. Now all you need to do is cut out the pattern.

If you want to transfer your template onto fabric, place the template onto the prepared, smooth reverse side of the fabric, and trace the outline with a pencil. You can then cut it out.

Iron-on interfacing

Some of the projects in the book work really well with iron-on interfacing. It 'sticks' two fabrics together, without the need for stitching.

First make a template of your pattern (see Making Templates). You can then transfer this onto fabric or craft felt. Cut out all the separate parts and trace them onto the paper side of the iron-on interfacing.

Then roughly cut everything out. Place the rough side of the interfacing onto the reverse side of the fabric, and dry-iron it for 3–4 seconds. Now carefully cut out your pattern and remove the non-adhesive paper.

Next place the piece of fabric in the correct position with the coated side facing down. Cover everything with a damp cloth and iron the piece of fabric for around 8–10 seconds, applying light pressure. Finally, leave the fabric flat to cool for 20 minutes.

In the run-up

Funky felt boots ★ Hanger buddies ★ Deluxe bird feeder
Cool Yule T-shirts ★ Pocket advent wreath ★ Snowman light
Snip-off calendar ★ Cuddly Christmas tree ★ Santa's surprises

Funky felt boots

Make Santa smile with these bright stockings

1. First make a template for your boot (see Making Templates). Then lay out two layers of felt, pin them together, trace the boot shape and cut it out.

2. You can now start to stitch evenly around the border. The easiest way to do this is with a sewing machine if you have one, but you can also use a sewing needle.

3. Next turn the boot inside out. Stitch a loop of satin ribbon to the back corner of the top edge of the boot.

4. Now comes the best part: decorating! Anything goes. You can attach ribbons, iron on motifs, and cut out felt Christmas trees, stars or flowers to glue in place. Now you have your own funky felt boot to display with pride!

Tip

A felt boot also makes excellent gift packaging for cookies, pens or homemade art – all sorts of things will fit inside.

Materials

- Craft felt in yellow, magenta, light green and turquoise, 3.5mm (⅛in) thick: 40 × 50cm (16 × 20in) for main boot shape and scraps for embellishments

- Satin ribbon in various colours, 6mm (¼in) wide, each 25cm (10in) long

- Scraps of ribbons and trims

- Pompoms in various colours and sizes

- Iron-on felt motifs

- Pins

- Sewing needle, or sewing machine (if available)

- Thread

- Scissors

- All-purpose glue

- Templates (see Templates)

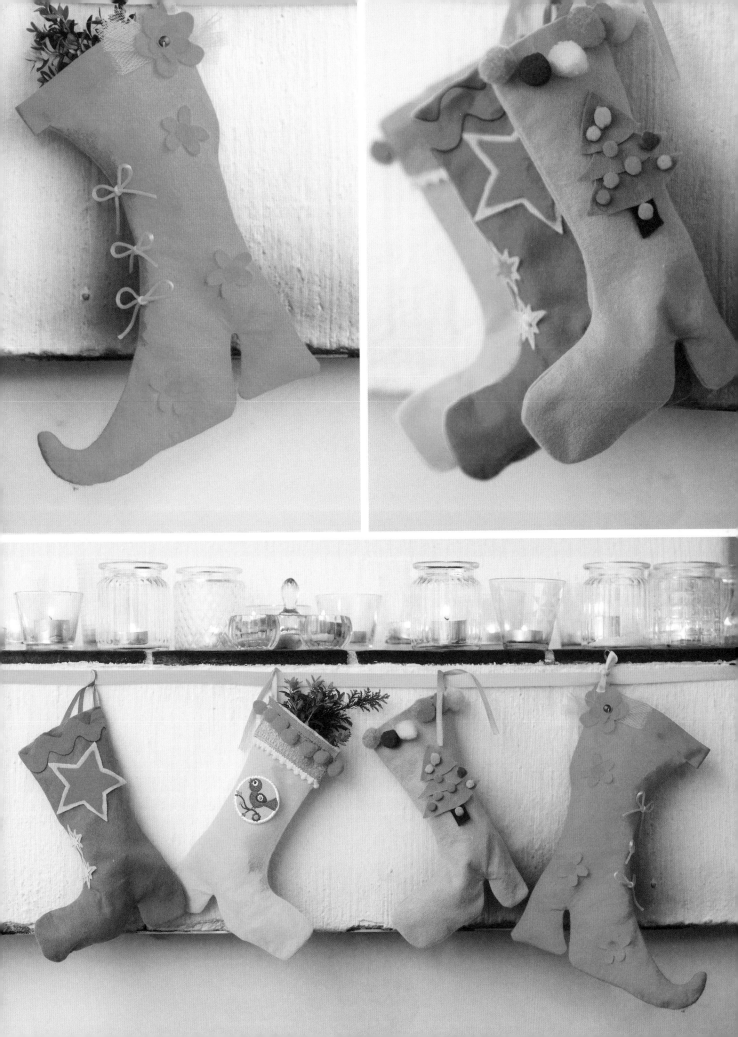

Hanger buddies

Fill their tummies with tasty treats!

1. First cut out a 1cm (³/₈in) wide strip from one side of each toilet roll. Cut open the resulting rings and attach them as handles on the left and right at one end of each toilet roll, using the stapler. Press the other end of each roll flat and staple them closed.

2. Now comes the painting: one roll red, one white and one yellow. First use a pencil to draw faces for Santa Claus and the angel then paint these areas pink.

3. Now you can cut out the separate parts for your hanger buddies from scraps of felt and stick them on as shown. For the angel, cut out the wings and a small mount for the star from glitter paper. Then continue to decorate them with Christmas-themed sequins.

4. Finally, paint funny faces onto the three figures. You can fill them with candy canes, chocolates or other little surprises.

Materials

- 3 empty toilet rolls
- Scraps of felt in white, yellow, pink, red, black and light blue
- Acrylic paint in white, yellow, red and pink
- Scraps of scrapbook paper and glitter paper
- Christmas sequin mix
- Felt-tip pens in red, black and blue
- Pencil
- Stapler
- Scissors
- Templates (see Templates)

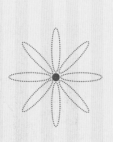

Tip

The hanger buddies are perfect for hanging on the Christmas tree, decorating gifts or dangling on your neighbour's door handle as a little token.

Deluxe bird feeder

★★★★★★★★★★★★★★★★★★★★★★★

Now the birds too can celebrate Christmas with a fancy meal

1. Before you start, make sure that you clean the drink carton thoroughly so that no left-over contents interfere with your handiwork. Then draw a window on the front and back of the carton. Leave a distance of at least 7cm (2¾in) between the base of the carton and the bottom of the window, so that you can pour in plenty of birdseed later.

2. Cut out the window using the craft knife. Now you can start painting. First apply a layer of light blue acrylic paint. Once this has dried, decorate the little house with white acrylic paint. Finally, you will need to paint your birdhouse with a layer of clear varnish to make it waterproof.

3. Snap the thin twigs into small pieces, making sure that all the pieces are around the same length. They should stick out a little from the edge of the drink carton. Now stick them to the top of the drink carton to make a roof using hot glue.

4. Saw off around 7cm (2¾in) from the handle end of a wooden paintbrush and paint it with white acrylic paint then clear varnish. Use the hole punch to make a hole in the centre of the carton, around 2cm (¾in) below the bottom of the window. Insert the wooden handle into the hole and stick it to the inside of the carton using hot glue.

5. Now you need to make the hanging bracket. To do this, use pointed scissors or a needle to make a hole at the centre of the top of the drink carton, thread the washing line through and knot the ends together. Finally, fill with birdseed and find a good place in a tree or bush to hang your bird feeder.

Materials

- Drink carton, 1 litre (1¾ pints)
- Acrylic paint in light blue and white
- Clear varnish
- Small twigs
- Rubberized washing line, around 50cm (20in) long
- Paintbrush with wooden handle
- Craft knife
- Hot-melt glue gun
- Hole punch, 8mm (³⁄₈in) in diameter
- Birdseed

Cool Yule T-Shirts

⭐⭐⭐⭐⭐⭐⭐⭐⭐⭐⭐⭐⭐⭐⭐⭐⭐⭐⭐⭐⭐

Your stylish new look for the festive season

1. First make templates of a snowman face and a reindeer face (see Making Templates). You can then transfer these onto your craft felt.

2. Cut out the separate parts and trace them onto the paper side of the iron-on interfacing. Roughly cut everything out. Now place the rough side of the interfacing onto the reverse side of the felt and dry-iron it for 3–4 seconds.

3. Cut out your pattern carefully and remove the non-adhesive paper. Next position the felt pieces correctly with the coated side facing down.

4. Cover everything with a damp cloth and then iron the piece of felt for around 8–10 seconds, applying light pressure. Iron on each part in this way until the pattern is complete. You should then leave your T-shirt lying flat for 20 minutes to cool before putting it on.

Materials

- T-shirts in white and green
- Craft felt in black, orange, light brown, dark brown, red, beige and light blue, each 20 × 30cm (8 × 12in)
- Iron-on interfacing (adhesive on both sides), 50 × 45cm (20 × 18in)
- Scissors
- Iron
- Template (see Templates)

Tip

Other great designs include a Christmas tree, snowflakes, an angel or simply the words 'Merry Christmas'!

Pocket
advent wreath

Can be used anywhere and everywhere

1. To make this ingenious pocket advent wreath, first paint the matchbox with acrylic paint in your favourite colour and leave until completely dry.

2. Then let your imagination run wild. You could stick on a Christmas tree, conjure up a paper star decoration or paint the box with an advent wreath. No doubt you will come up with plenty of other ideas!

3. Use the eyelet punch to put the four eyelets in the matchbox. This is where the candles will be placed.

4. Trim the birthday candles with scissors so that they are the right length to fit in the box. You may need to sharpen the ends a little with a sharpener before they will fit into the eyelets.

Materials

- Matchboxes
- Acrylic paint in magenta, yellow and light blue
- Eyelet punch and eyelets, 4.5mm (¼in) in diameter
- Scraps of coloured art paper
- Scraps of wrapping paper
- Birthday candles
- Scissors
- All-purpose glue

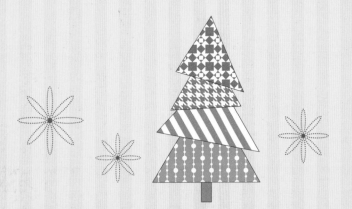

Tip

Now all you need to do is take out a candle and light it each week! First one, then two, then three, then four... then Christmas has arrived. At last!

Snowman light

★ ★ ★ ★ ★ ★ ★ ★ ★ ★ ★ ★ ★ ★ ★ ★ ★ ★

Guaranteed not to melt!

1. First paint the bottle with a layer of white acrylic varnish. Then cut off 5cm (2in) from the base using a craft knife. Press the bottle onto a polystyrene ring and cut more deeply in to the imprint with a craft knife so that the base of the bottle is firmly stuck in the ring.

2. Stick one chenille stem (pipe cleaner) around the bottom of the bottle. This will help to make it sturdier.

3. Now thread coloured pompoms onto the strand of wool with a needle. Tie a knot at each end of the thread first so that the pompoms don't slide down. Slide a larger pompom onto each end of the second chenille stem and bend the ends slightly to stop them from sliding down.

4. Now the snowman needs a face. Cut out five foam rubber circles for the mouth. Also cut out the eyes from foam rubber and make the nose with orange felt. Then stick on all the separate parts with all-purpose glue.

5. Stick one strip of double-sided sticky tape around the top of the bottle, around 8cm (3¼in) from the opening. Fold over the towelling fabric once on one of the long sides and then stick this side to the sticky tape.

6. You can now tie up the fabric above the head with a strand of wool to make the hat. All you need to do now is stick on the pompom earmuffs and your snowman is ready to use. Position the LED tea light in the centre of the polystyrene ring and turn it on.

Materials

- Plastic bottle, 1.5 litres (2¾ pints)
- White acrylic varnish
- Assorted pompoms, 2cm (¾in) in diameter
- 2 light blue pompoms, 4cm (1¾in) in diameter
- Polystyrene ring, 12cm (4¾in) in diameter
- Light blue towelling fabric, 15 × 25 cm (6 × 10in)
- 2 light blue chenille stems, 30cm (12in) long
- Black foam rubber, 10 × 20cm (4 × 8in)
- Scraps of orange felt
- Clear, double-sided sticky tape, 7mm (¼in) wide
- Wool strand, 45cm (18in) long
- Craft knife
- All-purpose glue
- Scissors
- Needle
- LED tea light
- Template (see Templates)

Tip

The LED tea light can of course be replaced with a bulb fitting containing a light bulb. And without the light, the snowman can be used as fun gift packaging!

Snip-off calendar

To keep you on track when counting down the days

1. First trim a strip of photo paper to 30cm (12in) long and 6cm (2½in) wide. Draw on 24 marks, each 1cm (³⁄₈in) apart.

2. Now stick scraps of fabric, washi tape, coloured sticky tape or woven ribbons onto each 1 × 6cm (³⁄₈ × 2¼in) area. Then write on the numbers 1 to 24 or cut them out and stick them on.

3. Cover the plastic stars with fabric. To do this, use the glue stick to attach each plastic star to the fabric and roughly cut it out. Cut notches in the edges of the fabric, fold them over and stick to the back.

4. Stick one star onto the photo paper above the 24, and the second star at a different angle on top of the first. Carefully cut off the remaining photo paper at the sides and decorate the star with the crocheted flower. Finally, attach a picture hook to the back of the star. Now 'snip off' a strip each day and you can always see how long there is left until Christmas.

Materials

- White photo paper, A4
- Washi tape, assorted patterns, 1cm (³⁄₈in) wide
- Scraps of fabric
- Patterned sticky tape, 1cm (³⁄₈in) wide
- Scraps of woven ribbons
- 2 plastic pendants: flat star, 9.5cm (3¾in) in diameter
- Crocheted flower
- Picture hook, 3.2cm (1¼in) in diameter
- Scissors
- All-purpose glue
- Glue stick

Cuddly Christmas tree

Snuggle up to this soft tree with secret wish list compartment

1. First copy the Christmas tree template (see Templates) to the desired size and transfer it onto the towelling fabric twice. Draw in seams 1cm (^{3}/$_8$in) around and then cut out along the outside line.

2. Draw the trunk onto the velour fabric, also with a 1cm (^{3}/$_8$in) seam, and cut it out. Cut the craft felt for the wish list compartment to the right size and stitch it to the centre of one side of the Christmas tree. Only stitch down the sides and the bottom, so that you can insert your wish list at the top.

3. Now cut out one large and one small star from craft felt, place these on the rough side of the interfacing and dry-iron for 3–4 seconds. Cut away the excess interfacing and remove the non-adhesive paper. Then place the stars (small star on top of the large star) in the desired position with the coated side facing down. Now cover everything with a damp cloth and iron for around 8–10 seconds, applying light pressure.

4. Now to assemble the cushion! First stitch the trunk to the towelling tree, placing the right sides together. Then place both sides of the Christmas tree with the right sides together and stitch them together. Leave a gap measuring around 8cm (3¼in) open on one side of the tree. Once you have finished stitching, turn the finished tree inside out through this gap so that it is now the right way around.

5. Stuff your tree with fibrefill. Finally, stitch the gap closed with a needle and green thread – and cuddle up!

Materials

- Light green towelling fabric, 120 × 60cm (48 × 24in)

- Green velour, 20 × 35cm (8 × 14in)

- Teal craft felt, 12cm (2¾in) square

- Craft felt in assorted colours, each 10cm (4in) square

- Fibrefill

- Iron-on interfacing, (adhesive on both sides) 50 × 45cm (20 × 18in)

- Sewing machine (if available)

- Sewing needle

- Green thread

- Scissors

- Template (see Templates)

Tip

Put your wish list in the secret compartment. It is certain to disappear at some point...

Santa's surprises

Beautifully packaged little gifts and treats

1. First transfer the template for the Santa Claus base, body and beard onto white photo paper and cut everything out. Then repeat the process for the belly using red photo paper.

2. Stick red felt to the white base body, so that the hat and arms later fit onto the belly. Stick black felt to the shoes. You can simply cut away any remnants.

3. Punch a hole in the centre of one of the short side walls of the removable matchbox drawer. It is best to do this with a sharp needle threaded with string. This means that you don't need to thread the strand through afterwards and you can immediately tie a knot inside the box to stop the string from sliding out. Thread a wooden bead onto the other end of the string and tie a knot there too.

4. Now slide the drawer back into the box and stick this to the Santa Claus base body.

5. Let's get decorating! Stick the red photo card belly to the front of the box. Then draw on a wide belt using a black felt-tip pen. You can make a buckle out of yellow felt and stick this onto the belt. Make two buttons out of yellow felt and glue in place, then stick the beard to the top part of the box. You can now give your Santa Claus a face.

6. Cut the small polystyrene ball in half using a craft knife, paint it pink and stick it on as a nose. Finally, cut the large polystyrene ball in half and stick it to the top of the hat as a bobble. And you're done!

Materials

- Matchbox, 11 × 6 × 2cm (4¼ × 2½ × ¾in)
- Red and white photo paper, A4
- Craft felt in yellow and black
- Polystyrene ball, 3cm (1¼in) in diameter
- Polystyrene ball, 1cm (³/₈in) in diameter
- Felt-tip pens in black, red and pink
- String or thread
- Wooden bead
- All-purpose glue
- Scissors
- Craft knife
- Sewing needle
- Template (see Templates)

Tip

Now you can think about the surprises in Santa's belly. Why not try chocolate balls, mini pens or stickers?

Good luck gifts

Glitter dough ★ Angel candles ★ Quirky badges
Glass magnets ★ Recycled crayon stars ★ Birdie handwarmer
Gorgeous gloves ★ Nativity box ★ Guardian angel

Glitter dough

Christmas kneading fun with an extra sparkle!

1. Mix the flour together with the salt and alum powder in a bowl. Heat up the water and add 45ml (3 tbsp) of oil. Then slowly pour this liquid into your flour and salt mixture.

2. Now you need to stir well until the dough is lukewarm. Divide the dough into five equally-sized portions. Then mix each of the food colourings with 5ml (1 tsp) of oil and about 10g (2 tbsp) of glitter. Wearing disposable gloves, knead them into the individual portions.

3. It is important that you keep your dough in an airtight container (e.g. a plastic bag), so that it stays soft for a long time.

Materials

- 400g (14oz) of flour
- 200g (7oz) of salt
- 10g (2 tbsp) of alum powder (available from pharmacies)
- 500ml (18fl oz) of boiling water
- 45ml (3 tbsp) of oil
- 25ml (5 tsp) of oil
- 15ml (1 tbsp) each of red, yellow, green and blue food colouring
- Tin of glitter
- Disposable gloves

Tip

Sculpt the dough into shapes and leave these to dry – they will become as hard as salt dough. You can also use a Christmas cookie cutter to cut shapes out of the dough straight away to make Christmas tree decorations.

Angel candles

Multicoloured dip-dying for heavenly effect

1. Dissolve the white wax together with the coloured wax crayons in a pan.

2. Now you can dip the tapered candles quickly into the wax to apply a layer of colour. You can dip them twice or even three times, depending on how intense you want the colour to be. Use more than one colour if you like.

3. Now leave everything to harden thoroughly.

4. Finally, cut out the angel wings from photo paper and stick the wings to the back of the candle using adhesive pads.

Materials

- 3 tapered candles

- White wax (e.g. 5 tea lights)

- Wax crayons (with a beeswax-based formula) in light blue, magenta and yellow

- Scraps of photo paper in light blue, pink and yellow

- Double-sided 3D adhesive pads, 3 × 2mm ($^1/_{16}$ × $^1/_8$in)

- Scissors

- Template (see Templates)

Tip

Why not write your own personal message on the wings before giving the candle as a gift?

Quirky badges

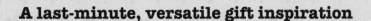

A last-minute, versatile gift inspiration

1. Place your bottle cap facing upwards on a pretty pattern on the wrapping paper. Now draw a circle around the bottle cap once with a pencil and cut out the pattern.

2. Stick the circle to a piece of photo paper and cut it out again. This will make it sturdier.

3. Now stick the pattern to the inside of the bottle cap and leave the whole thing to dry thoroughly. Then turn the bottle cap over and stick a brooch needle to the top. Your gift is ready to go!

Materials

- Bottle caps
- Brooch needles, 1.9cm (¾in) long
- Scraps of Christmas wrapping paper
- Scraps of photo paper
- Pencil
- All-purpose glue
- Scissors

Tip

You can make lots of these badges in next to no time. However, instead of sticking brooch needles to the back, you could also attach magnets and use them as fridge decorations.

Glass magnets

Ready in a jiffy!

1. Use a generous portion of all-purpose glue to stick the glass nuggets in the desired place on the wrapping paper. Leave to dry thoroughly.

2. Carefully cut away all the overhanging wrapping paper with the craft knife.

3. Finally, use all-purpose glue to stick the magnets to the back of the nuggets and leave to dry thoroughly again.

Materials

- Clear, transparent glass nuggets, 2cm (¾in) and 3cm (1¼in) in diameter

- Magnets, 1.5cm (⅝in) in diameter

- Scraps of wrapping paper

- Dry-clear all-purpose glue

- Scissors

- Craft knife

Tip

Parcel up a handful in pretty packaging and present them as a gift to your friends, parents or grandma!

Recycled crayon stars

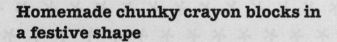

Homemade chunky crayon blocks in a festive shape

1. First you need to remove all of the bits of paper from the wax crayons. Then chop the crayons into smaller pieces with a knife and preheat the oven to 220°C (428°F/Gas Mark 7). If you like, you can sort the pieces of wax crayon according to colour.

2. Place the crayon pieces in the muffin moulds and put them in the oven for around 10 minutes. Wait until all of the wax has completely melted.

3. You can then carefully remove them (it is best to get an adult to help you to do this). Leave to cool thoroughly, until the whole thing has solidified into a hard block. Now you can press the new wax crayon stars out of the moulds.

Materials

- Wax crayons
- Silicone muffin moulds with Christmas motifs
- Knife
- Wooden board

Tip

Wrap together with a pretty wax crayon drawing to make a lovely gift!

Birdie handwarmer

A little friend to warm you up when it's icy cold

1. First make templates of your bird (see Making Templates), transfer them onto felt and cut them out. Cut out the wings from scraps of fabric. Place the rough side of the interfacing onto the reverse side of the fabric and dry-iron for 3–4 seconds.

2. Then carefully cut out the wing, remove the non-adhesive paper and place it in the desired position with the coated side facing down. Cover with a damp cloth and iron for 8–10 seconds.

3. Now you can stitch on the eyes. Stitch the hat to the head (with the right sides together). Try to make sure that both birds are lined up properly!

4. Next, place the bird with the wrong sides together and sew up the body. The easiest way to do this is with a sewing machine if you have one. Leave a gap of around 1.5cm ($^5/_8$in) open at the tail. Fill up with spelt kernels using a funnel through the gap, and stitch closed by hand using a needle and thread.

5. Iron the white bobble to the tip of the hat using interfacing in the same way as the wings.

Materials

- Craft felt in light green, pink, red and white, A4
- Colourful scraps of fabric
- Embroidery thread in light green and light blue
- Iron-on interfacing, (adhesive on both sides) 10 × 20cm (4 × 8in)
- Spelt kernels
- Thread
- Sewing machine (if available)
- Scissors
- Template (see Templates)

Tip

To heat up your handwarmer, place in the microwave for 30 seconds.

Gorgeous gloves

A cuddly, colourful gift to brighten up cold days

1. First make the template (see Making Templates). Fold your fleece fabric in half. Position the straight side of the template at the fold in your fabric. Now transfer the template onto your fleece fabric twice, leaving a 1cm (^{3}/8in) seam, and cut it out.

2. Arrange both gloves in front of you (still folded in half) so that one thumb points towards the right and one points towards the left. Then cut your woven ribbon to size and position it lengthwise down the centre of the front of your gloves. To make it easier to stitch down the ribbon, you need to pin it down. Fold back the ends of each woven ribbon at the top and bottom and pin them to the inside.

3. Now use the sewing machine to stitch straight along both sides of the woven ribbon edges. Your thread colour should match the colour of the woven ribbon. Make sure that the fleece fabric is no longer folded in two when you are stitching!

4. Then turn your gloves inside out. Now you can stitch together the side parts above and below the thumb. Turn the gloves the right way around again and you've made a cosy gift!

Materials

- Fleece fabric in light blue, white and pink, 40 × 90cm (16 × 36in)

- Woven ribbons, each 70cm (28in) long

- Sewing machine

- Pins

- Thread in matching colours

- Template (see Templates)

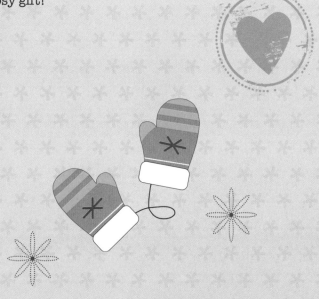

Nativity box

A traditional Christmas surprise

1. First cut out a rectangle from blue photo paper, the same size as the base of the box for the background, and stick it down.

2. Now let your imagination go wild and draw your nativity characters in pencil on white photo paper. Mary, Joseph, the baby Jesus, perhaps an angel, the ox and the ass, a stable – you are certain to come up with lots of ideas. Make sure that you leave enough distance between your characters.

3. Colour in all the characters with coloured pencils and cut them out. Make sure that you leave about 5mm (¼in) of photo paper at the bottom edge of each character. Bend this flap back.

4. Position the characters in the box as desired. Then apply a small amount of all-purpose glue to the photo paper flaps that you have folded over and stick down your characters where you want them to be placed.

5. Now you can make the lid for your nativity scene. Write a message for the person receiving the gift, tie it up with gift ribbon and you're done!

Materials

- White cardboard box, 22 × 14 × 6cm (8½ × 5½ × 2½in)

- 2 sheets of white photo paper, A4

- 1 sheet of blue photo paper, A4

- Coloured pencils

- All-purpose glue

- Pencil

- Scissors

- Gift ribbon

Guardian angel

She watches over us all Christmas long

1. Mix the paste according to the instructions on the packet. Then attach the cotton wool ball to the mouth of the bottle using masking tape.

2. Fold a piece of newspaper into a 3cm (1¼in) wide strip and cover the entire length with masking tape. Screw in a plastic cap at each end of the newspaper strips and secure these candle holders in place with masking tape.

3. Stick the candle holder arms at the centre of the back of the bottle with masking tape. Wrap a 15cm (6in) wide strip of newspaper once around the bottle underneath the arms and pad it out with newspaper to create a kind of skirt.

4. You can now paste everything (up to the head) with a layer of shredded newspaper. To do this, dip the shredded paper into the paste and spread it nice and flat onto the angel's body. The second layer is pasted with shredded copy paper.

5. Once everything is completely dry, you can start decorating. Paint the head pink, the top part of the body yellow, and the arms magenta. Then you can draw on the face. You can stick woven ribbons, a pompom border or other ribbons around the skirt, whatever you prefer.

6. For the hair, cut lots of wool strands to a length of around 20cm (8in) and then use all-purpose glue to stick them to the head. Cut out the wings using the template (see Making Templates) and stick them to the angel's back. Now you can insert the candles into the holders and present your work of art as a gift!

Materials

- Plastic bottle, 1.5 litres (2¾ pints)
- 1kg (2lb 4oz) of rice
- 2 plastic screw caps, around 1cm (³/₈in) in diameter
- 3 sheets of white copy paper, A4
- Cotton wool ball, 9cm (3½in) in diameter
- Newspaper
- Acrylic paint in yellow, red, magenta, black and pink
- Scraps of woven ribbon, pompom border and velvet ribbon
- Yellow photo paper, chequered, A4
- Yellow wool
- 2 candles
- Masking tape
- Paste
- All-purpose glue
- Template (see Templates)

Important!

Never leave your angel candle unattended when lit! You must also make sure that the candles are at a safe distance from the angel's head.

Confectionery

Jarful of delights ★ Santa Claus pancakes ★ Frilly angels
Chocolate cubes ★ Brownie shapes

Jarful of delights

All you need to bake your own heavenly treats

1. Fill the jar from bottom to top with the following ingredients in this order:

flour,
brown sugar,
chocolate beans,
brown sugar,
flour,
sugar,
chocolate chips,
rolled oats.

2. Now write out the following recipe on a nice piece of paper:

The only other ingredients needed for the recipe are 210g (7¼oz) of butter and 1 egg! Whisk together the egg and butter, then add the remaining ingredients. Chill the dough for two hours. Then preheat the oven to 180°C (400°F/Gas Mark 4) and line the baking tray with baking parchment. Shape the dough into walnut-sized balls, place them far apart from each other on the baking tray and bake for twelve minutes. Delicious!

Materials

- Jar, 1 litre (1¾pints)
- 120g (4¼oz) of brown sugar
- 60g (2¼oz) of granulated sugar
- 100g (3½oz) of rolled oats
- 150g (5½oz) of mini chocolate beans
- 100g (3½oz) of chocolate chips
- 270g (9¼oz) of flour

Tip

You can decorate the jar with fabric scraps, Christmas baubles and pretty ribbons.

Santa Claus pancakes

Father Christmas on a plate

1. Heat the butter and leave to cool down. Then mix together the flour and baking powder. Add the eggs, butter and milk and stir everything until you have a smooth batter. Fry the batter a portion at a time in the pan with butter, flipping it over to cook the other side.

2. Pour the cherries out of the jar, strain the cherry juice and mix with a tablespoon of cornflour. Heat the cherries and juice together, until the cherries are swimming in a thick sauce.

3. Now you can start decorating. Position a pancake in the centre of the plate. Use the cherries to make a hat. Then cut slices of banana for the eyes and put them in place. Make the pupils by placing cranberries onto the banana eyes. Finally, use spray cream to give your Santa Claus a beard and a bobble on his hat.

Enjoy!

Materials

Batter mix:

- 75g (2¾oz) of butter
- 2 eggs
- 250g (9oz) of flour
- 10g (2 tsp) of baking powder
- 75g (2¾oz) of sugar
- 300ml (½ pint) of milk
- 50g (1¾oz) of butter for frying

Also:

- A jar of cherries
- Banana
- Cranberries
- Spray cream
- Cornflour

Tip

Why not have a picnic under the Christmas tree? Spread out blankets and cushions and enjoy your pancakes with family or friends under the Christmas tree with candlelight and Christmas music.

Frilly angels

Almost too sweet to give away

1. Mix together the butter, sugar and egg, then add the flour. Knead the dough well and leave to chill in the fridge for at least one hour. Then roll out the dough onto a floured surface and cut out as many angels as you want using the cutter. Use the left-over dough to make the angels' hair.

2. Place all the angels onto baking parchment, slide the tray onto the middle shelf of the oven and bake everything at 200°C (400°F/Gas mark 6) for 15 minutes. Then mix the icing (confectioners') sugar with 5-10ml (1-2 tbsp) of water and a dash of red food colouring.

3. Use a paintbrush or kebab stick to paint on eyes and a mouth. Also use icing to 'stick' the chocolate bean decorations onto the dress.

4. Now you can decorate the angels! Cut out small pieces of doily and stick them to the angels' dresses with icing. Cut a muffin case in half with scissors and cut out wings for the angel from the semicircles. Stick these to the back with icing.

Materials

Dough mix:

- 200g (7oz) of butter
- 125g (4½oz) of sugar
- 1 egg
- 400g (14oz) of flour
- 150g (5½oz) of icing (confectioners') sugar
- Red food colouring
- Mini sugar pearls
- Coloured chocolate beans

Also:

- Angel cutter
- White doily
- Paper muffin cases
- Scissors
- Paintbrush or kebab stick

Chocolate cubes

The perfect gift for chocoholics

1. Melt the dark chocolate in a bain-marie (water bath) and stir in a teaspoon of cinnamon.

2. Melt the white chocolate in a bain-marie. Cut open the vanilla pod lengthways and scrape out the pulp with a knife. Then stir it into the white chocolate mixture.

3. Melt the milk chocolate in a bain-marie and flavour with two tablespoons of caramel syrup.

4. Now pour all the melted chocolate into an ice cube tray and stick a little plastic or wooden spoon into each cube. Decorate the different flavours with sugar sprinkles and leave everything to cool down and set.

Materials

- 150g (5½oz) of dark chocolate
- 150g (5½oz) of milk chocolate
- 150g (5½oz) of white chocolate
- Wooden or plastic spoons
- Ice cube tray
- Vanilla pod
- 5ml (1 tsp) of cinnamon
- 30ml (2 tbsp) of caramel syrup
- Decorative sugar sprinkles

Tip

The finished chocolate cubes are perfect for dipping in hot milk. But of course they're also delicious just as they are...

Brownie shapes

Framed chocolatey treats

1. First melt the milk and dark cooking chocolate and butter together and mix in two teaspoons of crème fraîche. Whilst doing this you can preheat the oven to 180°C (350°F/Gas Mark 4).

2. Now whisk the eggs with the sugar and then stir in the chocolate mixture. In another bowl, mix the flour, almonds, baking powder and cocoa and add everything to the chocolate mixture.

3. Line your baking tin with baking parchment and fill with the mixture. Now leave your brownies in the oven to bake for around 30–40 minutes.

4. Leave the brownies to cool down thoroughly and then remove them from the tin. Use a pallet knife to cut off the top surface from the brownies, so that you are left with a rectangle that is around 1.5cm (⅝in) high.

5. Now press the cutter into the surface of the brownie and then carefully remove it along with the contents.

6. Finally, fill the cutter shapes with melted chocolate, decorate with chocolate beans and leave to set.

Materials

- 150g (5½oz) of milk cooking chocolate
- 150g (5½oz) of dark cooking chocolate
- 100g (3½oz) of butter
- 10ml (2 tsp) of crème fraîche
- 3 eggs
- 200g (7oz) of brown sugar
- 150g (5½oz) of flour
- 22g (3 tbsp) of cocoa powder
- Pinch of salt
- 100g (3½oz) of ground almonds
- ½ sachet of baking powder
- 300g (10½oz) of milk chocolate
- Cutter shapes
- Chocolate beans
- Rectangular baking tin, 35 × 24cm (14 × 9½in)

Oh Christmas tree

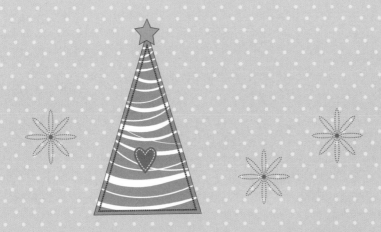

Glitter dinosaurs ★ Bell jar baubles ★ Jingle bells ★ Christmas owls
Ice blue flowers ★ Pretty snowflakes ★ Doily angels
Sparkling comets ★ Stripy Christmas trees ★ Jazzy straw stars

Glitter dinosaurs

Make your Christmas tree sparkle and roar!

1. First use the chestnut drill to make a hole at the centre of the top of your dinosaur and screw in the ring bolt. Then paint the dinosaur with varnish and leave to dry.

2. Now spray one dinosaur at a time with spray glue and use a spoon to sprinkle glitter over the top.

3. Thread a satin ribbon through the ring and knot the ends together. There you have it – a unique Christmas tree decoration.

Materials

- Plastic toys (dinosaurs)

- Acrylic varnish in yellow, light blue and light green

- Galvanized steel ring bolts, 10 × 3 × 1mm ($^3/_8$ × $^1/_8$ × $^1/_{16}$in)

- Chestnut drill, 2mm ($^1/_{16}$in) in diameter

- Glitter

- UHU spray glue

- Chequered decorative ribbon in yellow, green and blue, 5mm (¼in) wide, 20cm (8in) long

Bell jar baubles

A starring role for the pudding cup

1. Clean the pudding cup thoroughly so that you will be able to see through it properly later. Then use pointed scissors to make a hole in the base.

2. Thread the satin ribbon through a needle and knot the ends together. Now push the needle through the hole and cut the needle free with scissors. Knot the ends of the satin ribbon together again.

3. Arrange your plastic figurines as desired on the beer mat. Then place the cup over the top, making sure that all the parts have enough space around them.

4. Now you can stick your figurines to the beer mat with hot glue. Place the cup over the top again and stick the edges to the beer mat with all-purpose glue.

5. Finally, wrap the pompom border around bottom of the bell jar and stick down using all-purpose glue.

Materials

- Round beer mat, around 11cm (4¼in) in diameter

- Small plastic figurines (Christmas trees, mushrooms, people)

- An empty pudding cup, clear and with no imprint

- Pompom border, 9mm (³/₈in) wide, 30cm (12in) long

- Satin ribbon, 7mm (¼in) wide, 20cm (8in) long

- Hot-melt glue gun

- All-purpose glue

- Pointed scissors

Jingle bells

...Ring a ding ding!

1. Transfer the bell template onto the photo paper twice (see Making Templates) and cut them out. Coat both bells in all-purpose glue and stick them onto felt. Cut off the overhanging felt.

2. Now decorate. To do this stick ribbons, sequins, stars, buttons and so on to one side of the bell. Once you are happy with your work, stick together the two photo paper sides at the edges with all-purpose glue, leaving a gap at the top and bottom.

3. Take a piece of chequered ribbon and thread it through the small metal bell. Knot the ends together. All you need to do now is to thread the ribbon with the metal bell on it between the sides of the photo paper and you're done!

Materials

- Scraps of white photo paper

- Scraps of felt in various colours

- Ribbons

- Sequins

- Scatter stars

- Decorative gems

- Buttons

- Chequered decorative ribbon, 3mm (^{1}/$_8$in) wide, around 25cm (10in) long

- Small metal bell, 1cm (^{3}/$_8$in) in diameter

- Scissors

- All-purpose glue

- Template (see Templates)

Christmas owls

Cute fir cone birds with Santa hats

1. Paint the fir cones with acrylic paint. Also give the acorn caps a coat of white paint, adding a dot of black paint in the middle.

2. Cut a beak out of yellow felt and a circle with a 10cm (4in) diameter out of red felt. Cut the red felt circle in half for the hat. Then cut a strip around 5mm (¼in) wide and 10cm (4in) long out of white felt.

3. Attach the white strip to the round edge of the red semicircle. Bend the hat into a cone shape and fix the ends of the doubled-up satin ribbon to the tip. Now you can stick the hat together at the back.

4. Stick a pompom just below the point of the hat at the front.

5. Now you can use a hot-melt glue gun to stick on all the parts to the fir cone. Start with the eyes, because it is sometimes difficult to find a suitable place for them. Then attach the beak, the feathers and finally the hat. Now all you need to do is find a good place to hang your owls.

Materials

- Fir cones

- Acorn caps

- Feathers in various colours

- Scraps of craft felt in red, yellow and white

- Red satin ribbon, 1cm (³⁄₈in) wide, around 20cm (8in) long

- Acrylic paint in orange, light blue, green, yellow, magenta, black and white

- White pompom, 1cm (³⁄₈in) in diameter

- Hot-melt glue gun

Ice blue flowers

Create a winter wonderland in your home

1. First flatten the toilet rolls and use the craft knife to cut 6mm (¼in) wide sections (rings) from the short side. You will need six rings for each flower.

2. Brighten up the grey loo roll rings with acrylic paint. Leave them to dry thoroughly.

3. Arrange six ovals into a star shape and stick them together at the sides. To make sure that the whole thing holds together, you can use clothes pegs to pin each oval to the next until the glue has completely dried.

4. Now stick the underneath of the star to the photo paper and wait again until everything is dry. Use the craft knife to cut away the overhanging paper and stick a silver foil star in the centre of the flower.

5. Make a hole at the top of one of the ovals with a needle and thread through the embroidery thread. Thread on beads and sequins, tying a knot in between each one to stop the beads from sliding down. Finally, tie knots in the ends of the thread. And you're done!

Materials

- Toilet rolls
- Scraps of blue photo paper, A4
- Acrylic paint in various shades of blue
- Scraps of silver foil
- Blue beads
- Sequins
- Blue embroidery thread
- Needle
- Craft knife
- All-purpose glue
- Clothes pegs (optional)

Pretty snowflakes

Crochet patterned stars to add colour to the tree

1. First paint the paper coasters in lively colours. You will need two coasters for each decoration.

2. Fold the coaster in half, then fold again into a quarter. Now fold one more time, so that you have an eighth of a circle.

3. Take your scissors and cut pretty patterns into the side section. You can also cut into the curved edge. Take care not to damage the circle.

4. Now for the best part: carefully unfold the circle and admire your handiwork. Spray the unpainted side with spray glue and stick it onto the beer mat.

5. Make a hole in the edge of the beer mat with a needle, pull the thread through once and knot it. If you like, you can also thread on some beads.

Materials

- Round white paper coasters, 10cm (4in) in diameter
- A round white beer mat, around 11cm (4¼in) in diameter
- Acrylic paint in bright colours
- Beads (optional)
- Needle
- Thread
- Scissors
- UHU spray glue

Tip

The painted paper coasters are also perfect for decorating gifts.

Doily angels

Hark! The Herald Angels Sing

1. First paint the head of the wooden skittle in skin colour, and leave to dry thoroughly. Then you can paint on the hair, eyes, mouth and rosy cheeks with a thin paintbrush.

2. Cut a dress out of the doily using the template (see Making Templates). Apply all-purpose glue to the body, wrap the doily once around the body and stick it together at the back.

3. Tie the satin ribbon into small bows, shorten them to the desired length and press or iron them nice and flat. Now you can stick them to the neck.

4. Cut wings out of photo paper using the template and stick them to the angel's back with all-purpose glue.

5. Now use the chestnut drill to drill a hole at the centre of the top of the head. Screw the ring bolt into the hole. Cut a piece of decorative ribbon to the right size, thread it through the ring bolt and tie it in a knot. Now your angel is ready to hang...

Materials

- 3 wooden skittle figurines, 7cm (2¾in) high

- Doily

- Scraps of patterned photo paper

- Acrylic paint in red, magenta, skin colour, brown, yellow and black

- 3 ring bolts, 8 × 3mm (³⁄₈ × ¹⁄₈in)

- Satin ribbon in yellow, light green and light blue, 7mm (¼in) wide

- Chequered decorative ribbon in yellow, green and blue, 5mm (¼in) wide, 20cm (8in) long

- Chestnut drill, 2mm (¹⁄₁₆in) in diameter

- All-purpose glue

- Glue stick

- Template (see Templates)

Sparkling comets

Toothpicks as you've never seen them before!

1. First paint the polystyrene balls with acrylic paint. The best way to do this is to stick each ball onto a long kebab stick. This will allow you to paint them without getting paint on your fingers. Leave them to dry thoroughly.

2. Now start on the toothpicks. You will need around 24 toothpicks for each ball. Paint them with acrylic paint, stick the unpainted bottom points into a piece of floral foam and leave the toothpicks to dry.

3. Coat the polystyrene ball with clear varnish to give it a nice shine.

4. Use a needle to make holes in the polystyrene ball. Now push the toothpicks into the holes. Finally, stick a silver sequin onto the end of each toothpick.

5. Stick the ring bolt into the ball and thread through a satin ribbon. Now your comet is ready to sparkle!

Materials

- 5 polystyrene balls, 3cm (1¼in) in diameter

- Wooden toothpicks

- Orange satin ribbons, each 40cm (16in) long

- Silver sequins

- Acrylic paint in red, yellow, orange, light purple and dark purple

- Clear varnish

- 5 galvanized steel ring bolts, 10 × 3 × 1.8mm (³/₈ × ¹/₈ × ¹/₁₆in)

- Kebab sticks, 30cm (12in) long

- Floral foam

- Needle

Stripy Christmas trees

Rockin' Around the Christmas Tree...

1. First transfer the Christmas tree template onto white photo paper (see Making Templates). Then cut out the trees. Make a piece of satin ribbon into a loop and staple it to the back of the tree as a hanger.

2. Then stick the felt onto the tree trunk and cut away the overhanging parts.

3. Tear scraps of coloured fabric into 1cm (³/₈in) wide strips, or cut them out using the pinking shears.

4. Decorate the tree, starting at the bottom. Attach the first strip. Then stick on the second strip overlapping the first, and so on. Shorten the next strip at the sides each time to create a Christmas tree shape.

Materials

- White photo paper, A4
- Scraps of coloured fabric, 1cm (³/₈in) wide strips
- Light green craft felt, 15cm (6in) square
- Light green satin ribbon, 5mm (¼in) wide, 10cm (4in) long per tree
- Pinking shears
- Glue stick
- Stapler
- Template (see Templates)

Jazzy straw stars

**Turn something old into something new
– with jazzy colours!**

1. First paint the straw stars with colourful acrylic paint and leave
to dry thoroughly.

2. Stick a glossy picture in the centre of the front with
all-purpose glue – and your jazzy straw stars are done!

Materials

- Straw stars

- Acrylic paint in pink,
  light blue, orange, red,
  purple, blue, yellow
  and green

- Small glossy pictures

- All-purpose glue

Tip

These colourful straw stars
not only make perfect tree
decorations, but they are
also great for decorating
gifts. You can also stick
a label with a Christmas
message onto the back.

Playing around

Photo booth props ★ Memory game ★ Finger puppet nativity
Little angels ★ Rudolph reindeer

Photo booth props

All you will need for a cheeky winter photo shoot

1. First make templates for the dressing-up props (see Making Templates) and transfer them onto photo paper. Cut out all of the parts carefully with a craft knife.

2. You will need to stick together the separate parts for the carrot and the Santa hat.

3. Stick a kebab stick onto the back of each of your photo props with all-purpose glue. You can hold everything together with a clothes peg until it has dried properly.

4. Now all you need to do is get out your camera, find an attractive backdrop and have fun!

Materials

- A4 photo paper in white, red, black, light blue, light brown and orange

- Scraps of light green photo paper

- Clothes pegs

- Kebab sticks, 30cm (12in) long

- Craft knife

- All-purpose glue

- Templates (see Templates)

Tip

Print out the best photos and make them into Christmas postcards!

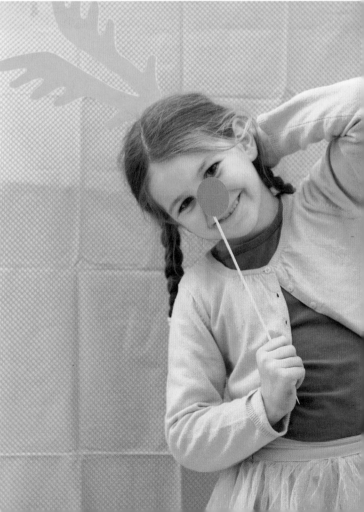

Memory game

Who is the brightest button in the box?

1. Draw 40 Christmas trees on green photo paper using the template (see Making Templates). You will need 20 of the smaller triangles in total. To make these, cut two triangles of each colour out of patterned photo paper. You could also use wrapping paper.

2. Carefully cut out all of the triangles. Then stick the green photo paper triangles together in pairs at the edges and bottom (leaving a gap around 1cm (³⁄₈in) wide at the bottom).

3. Now stick a smaller, coloured triangle onto each of the tree pairs. Then slide the lollipop stick between the two green tree halves through the gap in the bottom.

4. Now the game can begin. Turn all of the trees to 'green' and start to play!

Materials

- Light green photo paper, 50 × 70cm (20 × 28in)

- Patterned photo paper or wrapping paper, 20cm (8in) square

- Wooden lollipop sticks, around 18cm (7in) long

- Scissors

- All-purpose glue

- Template (see Templates)

Tip

You could also try other motifs such as stars, snowmen or bells. Can you think of anything else?

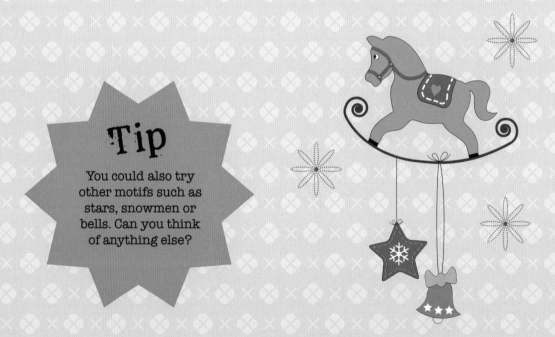

Finger puppet nativity

A nativity scene with a difference!

1. First cut the fingers off the rubber gloves – one after the other.

2. Then use the templates (see Making Templates) to draw the faces for Joseph, Mary, the baby Jesus, the shepherds and the three kings onto pink or light brown photo paper. Draw the sheep, the camel and the palm trees onto brown photo paper, and the star onto yellow photo paper. Now cut everything out.

3. Stick the palm trees onto green felt, cut off the overhanging fabric and stick a rubber fingertip onto the back. Attach the star to a kebab stick.

4. Stick each of the cut-out faces onto a rubber fingertip. Now you can put clothes on your characters. Cut dresses and cloaks out of scraps of felt and fabric and stick them around the rubber fingers with all-purpose glue.

5. You can also make hats, crowns, hair and moustaches, and decorate everything with borders, buttons and sequins. Let your imagination run wild!

6. Also decorate the sheep and the camel with fabric and felt. Stick on mini googly eyes and attach a rubber fingertip onto the back. Now you can start playing!

Materials

- 1 pair of rubber household gloves

- A4 photo paper in pink (or light brown), yellow and brown

- Scraps of felt

- Scraps of fabric

- Scraps of gold foil

- Scraps of velvet ribbon

- Googly eyes, 5mm (¼in) in diameter

- Buttons

- Sequins

- Scatter stars

- Kebab sticks

- All-purpose glue

- Scissors

- Templates (see Templates)

Little angels

Angel wings for cherubic cuddly toys

1. First copy the wing template to the desired size (see Making Templates) and then transfer the template onto the folded fabric, leaving a 1cm (³/₈in) seam.

2. Now cut out the wings twice. Place both pieces of fabric with the right sides together. Then stitch everything closed with the sewing machine, apart from a small hole around 8cm (3¼in) wide (see the marking on the template).

3. Turn the wings inside out through the hole so that they are now the right way around. You can use a kebab stick to straighten out the tips of the wings (use the non-pointy end).

4. You can now stuff the wings with fibrefill. Start with the tips of the wings. Use a kebab stick again to help you do this.

5. Once the wings are nice and plump, stitch closed the hole in the wings by hand (with a needle and thread). Stitch a brooch needle at the very centre of the wings so you can easily attach them on to a cuddly toy.

Materials

- White cotton, 60 × 40cm (24 × 16in)
- Fibrefill
- Brooch needle, 1.9cm (¾in) long
- Sewing machine
- Pins
- Needle
- Thread
- Scissors
- Kebab sticks
- Template (see Templates)

Tip

If you are making the wings for your dolls, simply stitch two elastic band loops and attach these to the wings. You can then put the wings onto the doll like a rucksack.

Rudolph reindeer

A hand puppet to fall in love with

1. First cut the beer mat in half. Turn the Norwegian sock inside out and create a dent in the front. Stick the beer mat halves to the top and bottom of the dent with all-purpose glue. Leave to dry thoroughly and then turn the sock the right way around again.

2. Now cut a third off both the polystyrene balls using a craft knife. Use a permanent marker to draw pupils onto the polystyrene balls and stick them to the heel of the sock with all-purpose glue.

3. Sew on the red pompom for the nose using a needle and thread.

4. Now for the antlers. Transfer the template (see Making Templates) onto brown photo paper and carefully cut them out. Staple both the antlers together at the bottom centre, reinforce with a circle of brown craft felt and stick them in place.

5. Finally, stuff Rudolph with some fibrefill. Now all you need to do is put your hand in the sock and you're ready to go.

Materials

- Norwegian sock
- Round beer mat, around 11cm (4³⁄₈in) in diameter
- 2 polystyrene balls, 4cm (1½in) in diameter
- Red pompom, 4cm (1½in) in diameter
- Brown photo paper, A4
- Scraps of brown craft felt
- Fibrefill
- Permanent marker
- Sewing needle
- Thread
- Craft knife
- All-purpose glue
- Scissors
- Stapler
- Template (see Templates)

New Year's Eve crackers

Confetti cannon ★ Lucky clover bubbles ★ Party hats

Confetti cannon

A brightly-coloured firework to bring the New Year in

1. Transfer the template (see Making Templates) onto the glitter paper and cut it out. Then roll it into a cone at one edge. The opening at the bottom should be around the same size as the end of the balloon pump.

2. Staple the overlapping paper strips together at the larger opening. Seal the rest of the seam with hot glue.

3. Cut a circle out of aluminium foil and use it to cover the small opening. Stick down the edges of the foil with a glue stick.

4. Insert a funnel into the larger opening of the confetti cannon and fill with confetti. You can use a kebab stick or a pencil to push it in. Cover this end too with an aluminium foil circle – you will only need to do this if you don't want to use your confetti cannon straight away, to prevent the confetti from falling out.

5. And now for the confetti fun: extend the balloon pump and place the small opening of your cannon onto the pump outlet. Hold on tight to the confetti cannon and push the pump together with the other hand. Now you can welcome in the New Year with a fantastic shower of confetti. Happy New Year!

Materials

- Scrapbook paper: glitter, iridescent
- Confetti
- Aluminium foil
- Balloon pump
- Funnel
- Scissors
- Stapler
- Hot-melt glue gun
- Glue stick
- Template (see Templates)

Tip

You can reload your cannon as many times as you like, so you can cover all your friends and family with a confetti shower!

Lucky
clover bubbles

The perfect lucky charm gift!

1. Take the chenille stem (pipe cleaner) and bend 20cm (8in) of it into a circle. Bend the circle end once around the 10cm (4in) long handle using pliers.

2. Now use the pliers to bend the circle into four equal quarters. You will need to tightly press together the dents created with the pliers.

3. Then repeat exactly the same steps inside the curved parts to make a clover leaf shape.

4. You can paint the jar lid with red acrylic paint and leave it to dry. Use the hot-melt glue gun to stick a red and white mushroom onto the centre of the top of the lid.

5. Now carefully mix the ingredients to make your soap bubble liquid. Once there is no more foam, the soap bubble mixture can be poured into the jar and is ready to use. Can you blow a lucky soap bubble?

Materials

- Jar with lid

- Chenille stem 6mm (¼in) in diameter, 30cm (12in) long

- Wooden red and white mushrooms

- Red acrylic paint

- Hot-melt glue gun

- Pliers

- Template (see Templates)

Soap bubble recipe:

- 115ml (3¾fl oz) of washing-up liquid, clear and colourless

- 15ml (1 tbsp) of glycerine

- 1.5 litres (2¾ pints) of water

- Template (see Templates)

Party hats

It's time to party in these colourful cone hats!

1. Cut out the basic shape of the hat from patterned photo paper using the template (see Making Templates). Leave the crêpe paper rolled up and cut off a 2cm (¾in) strip wide from the end of the roll. Cut off a 1.5cm (⅝in) wide strip from the other colour in the same way.

2. Place the resulting crêpe paper rolls together and make a little snip every 5mm (¼in) on both sides. You can then fold them out.

3. Place two layers of each colour on top of one another and then staple all four layers together to the bottom round edge of the hat. Fold the crêpe garland down so that it hides the staples.

4. Use the needle to make two small holes in the photo paper; one on either side. Then thread the elastic from the inside to the outside through one hole and back through the other. Finally, knot it in place, also knotting the other end.

5. Now roll the hat into shape, leaving around 1cm (³/₈in) overlapping, and staple together at the overlapping part.

6. For the pompom at the tip of the hat, thread the needle and thread back and forth through the centre of a left-over crêpe strip measuring 10cm (4in). String the whole thing onto the thread and push right into the end of the knots. Tie the bottom part with the thread and knot it. Pull the pompom apart at the top (it should now look like a bunch of flowers) and stick it into the hole at the top of the hat.

Materials

- Blue, yellow and red crêpe paper, 0.5 × 2.5m (1½ × 8¼ft)

- Patterned photo paper, A4

- Transparent elastic thread, 0.5mm (¹/₃₂in) in diameter, 30cm (12in) long

- Stapler

- Scissors

- Needle

- Thread

- All-purpose glue

- Template (see Templates)

Templates

Some of the templates are shown
at 50% size and need to be enlarged
by 200% where marked.

Hanger buddies

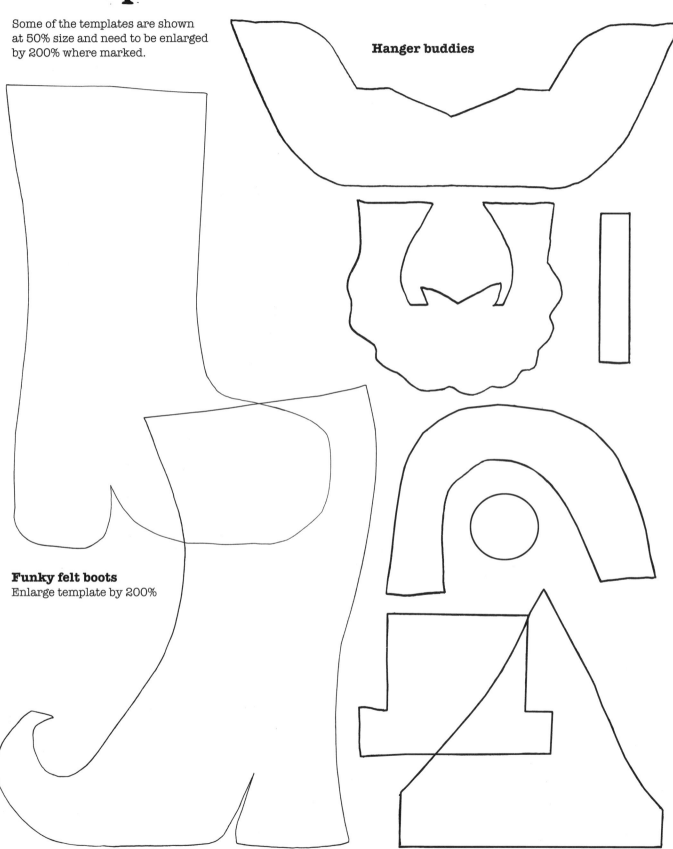

Funky felt boots
Enlarge template by 200%

Cool Yule T-shirts
Enlarge template by 200%

Cuddly Christmas tree
Enlarge template by 200%

Snowman light

Birdie handwarmer

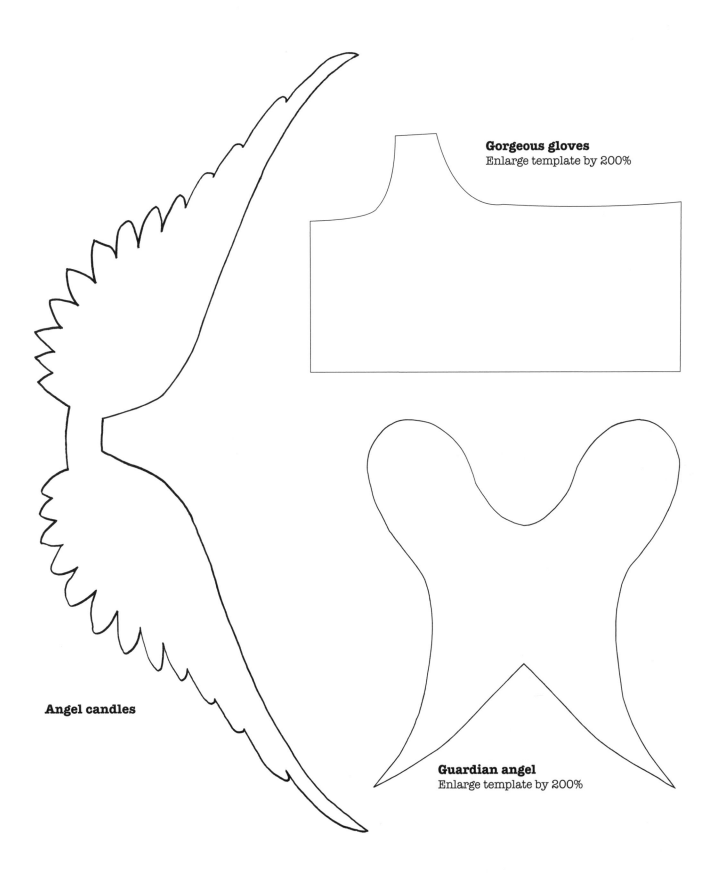

Gorgeous gloves
Enlarge template by 200%

Angel candles

Guardian angel
Enlarge template by 200%

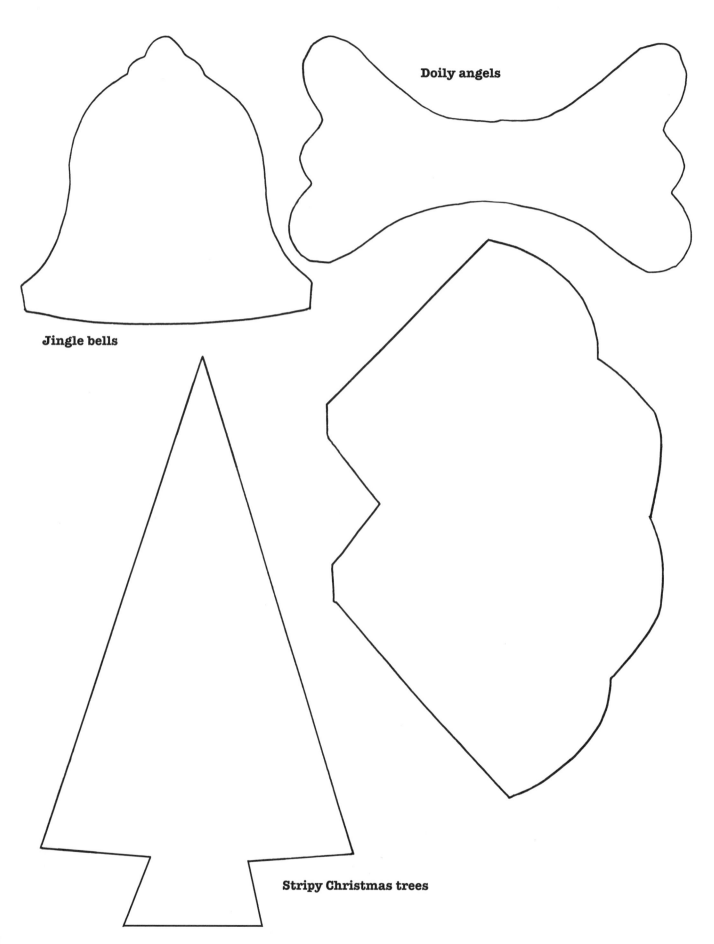

Doily angels

Jingle bells

Stripy Christmas trees

104

Photo booth props
Enlarge templates by 200%

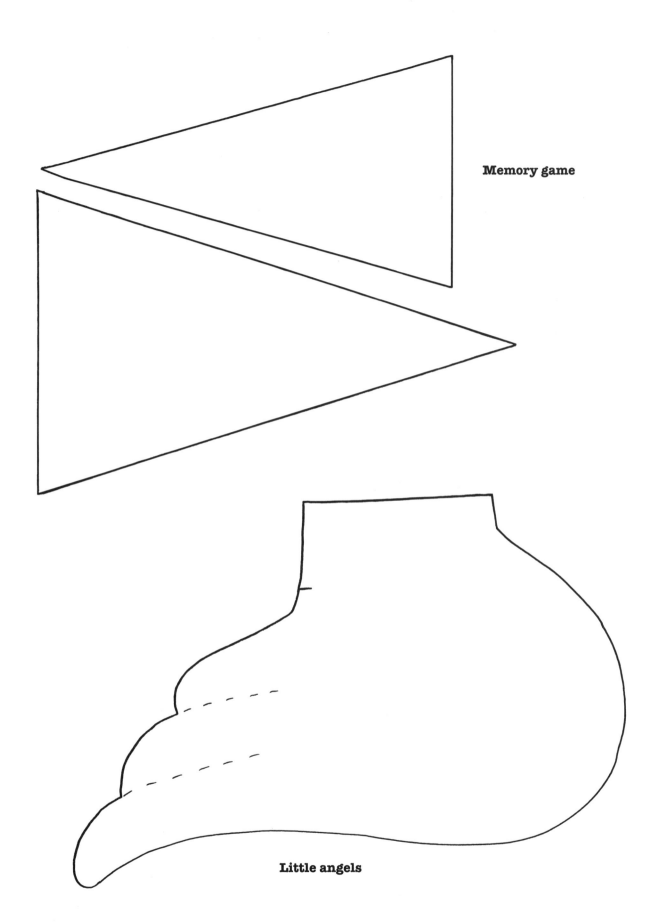

Memory game

Little angels

Rudolph reindeer

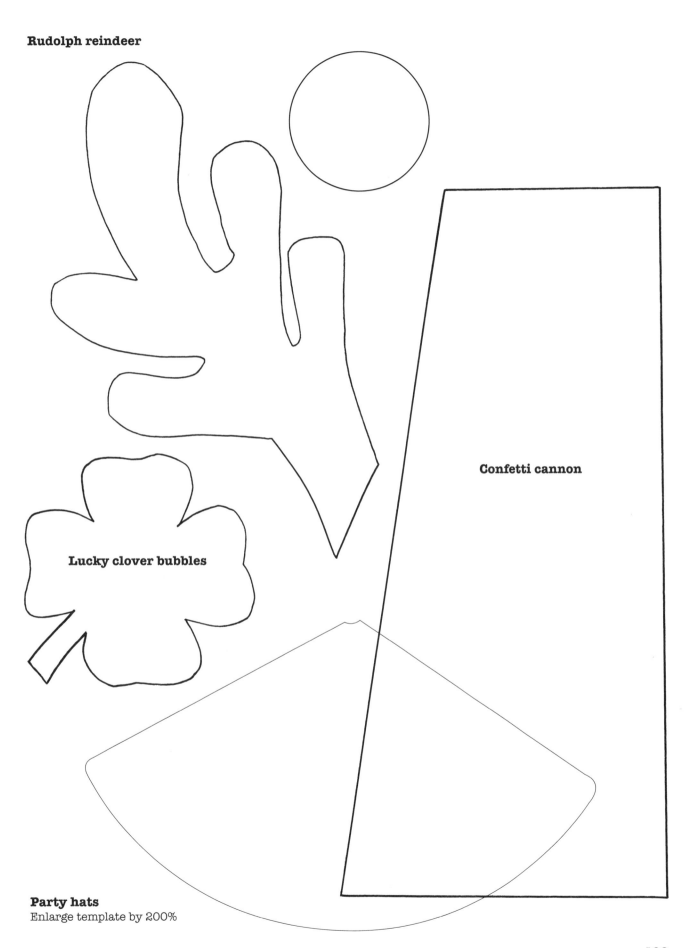

Confetti cannon

Lucky clover bubbles

Party hats
Enlarge template by 200%

About the Author

Pia Deges has written four previous books, with the latest 'Mädchenglück' published in January 2013. Although she studied film and television and now writes for television, she much prefers to play with fabric, paper, scissors and glue, making crafts for all occasions. She lives with her family in Essen, Germany.

Acknowledgements

Opening parcels from the following companies was like Christmas every time for me. My sincere thanks go to Heyda (Heilbronn), Rico Design (Brakel), Efco (Rohrbach), Rayher (Laupheim), Knorr-Prandell (Lichtenfels) and RBV Birkmann (Halle/Westphalia) for their wonderful support!

Celebrating Christmas in May wouldn't have been half as much fun without Olivia, Oskar, Felix, Emil, Ida, Katha, Michael and Angela. Thanks very much to all of you!

Index

A DAVID & CHARLES BOOK
© frechverlag GmbH 2012

Originally published in Germany as Knallbunte Weihnachten

First published in the UK and USA in 2013 by F&W Media International, Ltd

David & Charles is an imprint of F&W Media International, Ltd
Brunel House, Forde Close, Newton Abbot, TQ12 4PU, UK

F&W Media International, Ltd is a subsidiary of F+W Media, Inc
10151 Carver Road, Suite #200, Blue Ash, OH 45242, USA

A catalogue record for this book is available from the British Library.

ISBN-13: 978-1-4463-0384-9 paperback
ISBN-10: 1-4463-0384-5 paperback

Printed in China by RR Donnelley for:
F&W Media International, Ltd
Brunel House, Forde Close, Newton Abbot, TQ12 4PU, UK

10 9 8 7 6 5 4 3 2 1

Photos: frechverlag GmbH, 70499 Stuttgart; lichtpunkt, Michael Ruder, Stuttgart
Layout, composition and illustrations: Melanie Dahmen
Product management: Angela Vornefeld
Editing: Alice Hörnecke and Angela Vornefeld

F+W Media publishes high quality books on a wide range of subjects.
For more great book ideas visit: www.stitchcraftcreate.co.uk